YOU GOT INTO WHERE?

How I Received Admission and Scholarships to
the Nation's Top Universities

YOU GOT INTO WHERE?

How I Received Admission and Scholarships to
the Nation's Top Universities

JOI WADE

Joi Wade
2016

First Printing: 2016

ISBN-13: 978-1-365-15971-8

Published by Joi Wade
3645 Marketplace Blvd. STE-130-302
Eastpoint, Georgia 30344

www.joiwade.com

Library of Congress Cataloging-in-Publication Data

Cover Design by Joi Wade

This book is available at quantity discounts for bulk purchases. For information please send an e-mail to joiwadeinquiries@gmail.com.

For my parents, Cynthia and Maurice, who supported me every step of the way through my college application process.

Contents

WHY I WROTE THIS BOOK

As an underclassman in high school, I always wondered how students gained admission to top universities. As a first-generation college student, I had to go the extra mile to seek guidance to get into college. Every night after school I researched college application tips and guidelines: I read blogs, e-mailed admissions officers, watched videos, and purchased and pored over books. My friends thought I was insane because of how determined I was to get into college. Even though I had good grades, I wanted to make sure I did everything in my power to attend my dream university.

During my senior year, I used my YouTube channel as an outlet to share the knowledge I was acquiring on college admissions. I produced videos on ACT advice, admissions interviews, and other aspects of the college application and admission process. As I went on college and university tours, I recorded videos of each campus and shared them with my growing audience. I realized that so many students did not have the resources available to them to learn about the college preparation and application process, and I wanted to share all I knew so I could help them in the best way.

When college admission decision time rolled around for me, I continued to share my experiences through "admission decision reaction" videos, in which I opened each of my college admission response letters. I took my viewers along with me to my scholarship interviews. Finally, I announced my decision to join the University of Southern California's Class of 2020.

The feedback I received from my videos was overwhelming. Everyday students messaged me on social media, congratulating me on my acceptances. Students flooded me with their own admissions questions and wanted my advice. I was so happy to be able to respond to them with my personal advice based on my personal experiences.

During those final stages of my college admission process, I knew I had to share the knowledge I had attained so I could help others to be as successful as I was. I wanted another outlet beyond YouTube and blog posts, so I decided to write this book, which shares the full story of my college preparation, application and admission process through facts, tips, and personal anecdotes.

I believe we must gain information about a topic from many different viewpoints. College application season is a confusing time for many high-school seniors, and hundreds of articles flood the Internet about the "right" and "wrong" ways to tackle getting into college.

While it was important for me to read the expert opinions from admissions officers and counselors, some of the most valuable counsel I learned during my college application process came from students who had recently enrolled in college. I communicated with them through social media and e-mail and during my campus visits. I felt as though I could really connect with these students, because they knew what I was going through. They were not adults who had graduated 20 years ago—they were my peers who still remembered the pain of taking the SAT and completing the perfect Common Application essay.

I hope that, through this book, I can communicate just as effectively to my readers. Though I am no college admissions guru, I believe that my experience-based perspective will enable students to learn more about, and become confident in, their ability to prepare for and apply to college most effectively. By using this book in combination with other resources, you can have a tool-belt of information ready to go when you enter the college application realm.

Your **student** mentor,

Joi Wade

Joi Wade

Disclaimer: I am not a college admissions expert or admissions officer. This book is intended as a guide to help students learn about the college preparation and application process from the perspective of a student who recently went through it successfully. Following the advice given in this book does not guarantee admission or scholarships to any post-secondary school institution. For professional guidance, seek the advice of a college admissions officer, your high-school counselor, or a professional college advisor.

HOW TO USE THIS BOOK

Imagine me as one of your older friends who have just decided which colleges or universities they will attend. While you know I have no experience in college admissions, you nevertheless want to know about the process I went through to get to where I am now. Let this book be your insider's guide to the methods I used to apply to college.

Feel free to jump around from chapter to chapter based on the information you need to know at this point in your college preparation and application process, whether you are a freshman, a sophomore, or a junior going into your senior year.

Finally, make sure you reference the appendix and resources I provide in the back of the book. Here you will find a copy of my admissions essay, supplement, activities resume, and more. I also provide worksheets and guides to help you along the way. You can further expand your knowledge of the college admissions process by checking out some of the books, websites and scholarship sources I recommend. Even more resources—blog posts, videos, printable materials, etc.—can be found on my website, JoiWade.com.

CHAPTER 1

GETTING READY

Unfathomable as it may seem, the college preparation process begins as soon as you matriculate into high school. From scheduling courses to taking on extracurricular activities, every choice you make during your first three years of high school will factor into your college applications, acceptances and final selection.

Courses to Take

Each high school offers a wide variety of courses in a diversity of subjects. Most schools offer courses at all learning levels from Basic to Standard to Honors. Some have college-level Advanced Placement (AP) or International Baccalaureate (IB) options, through which students can earn college credit so they can take reduced course loads in college, or even graduate early to save tuition money. When deciding which courses to take, the main thing to consider is their level of rigor. You must ask yourself, "Am I taking the hardest possible course load, and will I be able to be successful in these courses?" It is important not to bite off more than you can comfortably chew. But it is equally important not to slack, simply because you want a school year of easy classes.

After all, when college admissions officers look at your transcript, they study the courses you were and are currently enrolled in. They compare the number of AP/Honors/IB courses you have taken to how many are actually offered at your school. If an admissions person sees that you took only two AP courses throughout your three years of high school, but your school offers fifteen, they may wonder why you chose not to take on that extra challenge. Furthermore, a higher number of AP/Honors/IB courses on your transcript will improve your chances of acceptance at a college of high academic reputation where admissions are more competitive.

Special Educational Experiences

Dual Enrollment: Dual-enrollment courses are college courses offered to high-school students to gain pre-matriculation college credit. They are a great option if your school does not offer AP or IB programs. Dual enrollment is also a great way to continue to exercise rigor on your high-school transcript if you have completed all of your school's AP/IB courses. Before signing up for dual-enrollment classes, however, I suggest you find out whether your top-choice schools accept credit through dual enrollment, and whether they prefer AP or IB courses over dual-enrollment ones.

Summer Programs and Courses: Almost every college and university offers opportunities for high-school students to come to campus in the summer and take courses. These programs can be expensive, but they are a great way for you to get a preliminary feel for college campus life and to continue your academic enrichment throughout the summer. If you cannot afford an expensive summer-school program or do not wish to travel far for one, I suggest looking into smaller local colleges that offer such programs.

Study Abroad: Programs for study abroad in foreign countries are being expanded into the high-school years. AFS and other intercultural programs now enable high-school students to spend a summer, semester or academic year in the country of their choice to gain high-school credit, sometimes offering scholarships for that purpose. Studying abroad is a great way for students to experience new cultures, broaden their perspectives, and get away from their daily life and school routines. Experiences in foreign nations also inspire phenomenal college application essays.

If you plan to study abroad, make sure your high school will award credit for your studies. You certainly would not want to have to repeat a grade because your courses in Thailand do not translate into the American school system.

Grades and GPA

A key factor in admission to the college of your choice is your grades. Admissions officers want to see that you are succeeding in your academic courses so they can feel confident that you will do well at their college or university.

Many students wonder if they should tackle an AP course, because they're worried about getting a lower grade in it than they would get in a regular course on that subject. As I mentioned earlier, AP holds a lot of weight on your application. So I do encourage everyone to take an AP course and get a "B" rather than go for an "A" in the Honors, Standard or Basic equivalent.

Also important in college admissions is the difference between an "unweighted" and a "weighted" grade point average (GPA). Unweighted GPAs are mostly on the 4.0 scale. However, schools may add "weight" to Honors and AP courses to balance their rigor levels and the grades you received in them against those of your less demanding courses. So a weighted GPA may end up on a scale of 7.00, or you may just have points added to your final semester grade in the AP or Honors course.

Class Rank

Your class rank lets a college see where you stand in the context of your high-school peers. Even if you are not your class valedictorian, your rank in class still indicates how you perform in your school. Class rank calculation varies from school to school: some use weighted GPA, others unweighted GPA, to determine where students stand in relation to their peers. If your school does compute class rank, a good goal for you is to aim for the top 25% in your class for less selective schools and the top 10% (or higher) if you are applying to more selective colleges. If your school does not use class rank, an admissions officer will be aware of this, and it will not hurt you in your application, for your GPA and your number of AP/Honors/IB courses will still carry weight.

Extracurricular Activities

Many high-school students applying for college are inclined to join every single club they can find in their school to fill up their resume and make a splash impression on the college admissions people. This is the exact opposite of what needs to happen.

Quality, Not Quantity: Colleges look for depth, not breadth, in a student's extracurricular activities. In other words, you want to specialize in a few things rather than place yourself all over the place. As an example, in the back of this book you will find my activities resume (see Appendix B). Throughout high school, I knew I wanted to apply to colleges and universities with communications and journalism-related majors, so I made sure that most of my clubs and activities dealt with my major in some way. For example, I was an anchor for the morning announcements, a writer for the school newspaper, and an editor for the yearbook. So I was involved in a lot of things at my school, but when they appeared on my activities list, an admissions officer could tell what type of person I was and where my interests lay.

I therefore advise anyone to choose a specific focus for their extracurriculars. The college application is about creating an overshadowing message about yourself, your interests and your strengths, so admissions officers can remember who you are and what you do best. If you have a lot of random items on your application, it makes it harder for them to picture your place on their campus. (Furthermore, an extracurricular overload may limit your study time, which could lower your grades, leaving admissions officers with an even less good impression of you.) The specific activities you wish to pursue do not matter as much as your demonstration of your passion for and involvement in those pursuits.

If a club means a lot to you that does not relate to your major, and you believe you are making a positive impact in it, then definitely take your place in that club. But you must also pursue activities that genuinely interest you. I was a Varsity swimmer and participated heavily in volunteer activities, just because I loved doing them.

Remember: you do not have to be in everything. Finding a few activities that give you pleasure and enable you to emerge as a leader in the group is all that matters.

Leadership Positions: When talking about extracurriculars in the college admissions realm, many people emphasize taking on leadership positions in clubs and organizations. While this may include being elected a club president or treasurer, there are many other ways to show leadership and dedication to your activities. Consider organizing a fundraiser or event, designing promotions, taking down club minutes, or any other helpful task in your organization.

Starting a Club: A great way to show initiative and leadership is to start your own club or organization. If you are passionate about a hobby or cause, this is a great way to bring together people of similar interests. As your club's founder, you will be in charge of recruiting members, planning meetings and activities for them, and thereby making a change in your school or community. If you are interested, brainstorm about the purpose and activities of your club and write a proposal to your school principal for approval.

Community Service: Your high school may already require you to complete community service hours to graduate. Regardless, community service is a great way to meet new people and help those in need. Whether you tutor middle-school students, volunteer at a local hospital, or prepare and serve meals in a homeless shelter, there are an abundance of ways you can lend a helping hand in your community. By participating in these activities, you show that you care about more than yourself and truly want to make a difference in the lives of others.

Out-of-School Activities: If you are having trouble finding the right activity for you within your school, seek organizations in your community that offer spots for high-school students. Activities outside of school can include internships, work experience, and volunteering.

CHAPTER 2

EXAMS, EXAMS, EXAMS

Some of the most stressful aspects of college admissions are the required standardized exams. Every year, high-school students get anxious over their test scores on the infamous SAT and ACT tests, which they usually take in their junior year so their scores can be part of their college application package. While test scores are not the be-all and end-all of your application, it helps to be prepared and go into the test confident you can do your very best.

In the spring of my junior year, I took the previous version of the SAT (in March 2016, the College Board released its new version) and scored 1730/2400, which was not bad, but not where my score needed to be to apply to the selective colleges of my choice. I thus decided to take the ACT as well. I received a 29 composite score the first, second and third times I took the test. My fourth shot at the ACT gave me what I was praying for—a 31.

Many students score better on one test over the other—in my case, the ACT. For others, their scores come out pretty even between the two. Either way, I recommend you take each test once without preparing heavily, and whichever one you score higher on should be the test to focus on. Once you find which test fits you, take the time to prepare for it so your scores can improve.

About the PSAT and the PLAN

The Preliminary Scholastic Aptitude Test/National Merit Scholarship Qualifying Test (PSAT/NMSQT) is a mock-SAT, usually taken in the fall of a student's sophomore year. This exam is shorter than the SAT and allows students to get comfortable with the testing format. PSAT test-takers also compete during their junior year to be named National Merit Scholars, or at least Finalists, Semi-finalists or Commended Students. Only those who receive phenomenal scores are named National Merit Scholars; these students may have many scholarship opportunities available to them from the National Merit Scholarship Corporation and many other universities. PSAT scores are not part of college admissions criteria, although receiving a Letter of Commendation or a Certificate of Merit as a Finalist is an honor worth mentioning on your application.

The PLAN is similar to the PSAT and is taken during a student's sophomore year as a rough prediction of how that student will score on the ACT test.

About the SAT

The Scholastic Aptitude Test (SAT) released a new testing format in 2016. The new SAT has: (1) reading, (2) writing and language, and (3) math sections, totaling a time of 3 hours, with an optional 50-minute essay. The exam is scored on a range of 400-1600 points. The SAT is offered seven times a year; registration deadlines are usually about four weeks before the test date.

About the ACT

The ACT (American College Testing) exam has reading, English, math and science components, totaling a time of 2 hours and 55 minutes, with an optional 40-minute essay. The exam is scored on a range of 1-36 as a composite score. The ACT is offered six times a year; registration deadlines are usually five weeks before the test date.

Studying for the Tests

Many resources are available to help you improve your score, including websites, books, and tutors. I used a tutor for a couple of sessions so I could pinpoint where I was losing points and have guided practice in those areas so I wouldn't make those mistakes again. If you are unable to hire a tutor, find free practice tests online and complete them. If you are particularly weak in the math section, take your time and work out the problems you miss often. If you are a slow reader and can never finish the passages in time, work on timed reading sections until you can finish early.

Practice is important. I had to take the ACT four times, because I did not do enough preparation the first few times around. Once I dedicated the time and energy for preparations, my composite scores improved from 29 to 31.

Setting up a weekly study regime will help you stay on track to mastering the skills necessary to improve your score.

Registering for the Tests

Both the SAT and the ACT require you to register online, and you must register early enough so testing locations close to you do not fill up. First, you fill out a profile with basic information about yourself and your school. Then you can select your preferred test date and location. You will also be prompted to upload a photo of yourself to be used on your admission ticket on test day. Finally, you pay the fee or submit a fee waiver, which is available from your high school's guidance office if you are eligible for it.

Test Day

It is crucial to set yourself up for success the day you are taking your test. Make sure you get a good night's sleep, eat a healthy breakfast, and allow enough time to get to your testing center to check in and use the restroom. Bring with you:

1. your testing ticket (which you must print out);

2. a bunch of sharpened #2 pencils with erasers;

3. an approved calculator;

4. snacks and water for break-time;

5. notes on testing strategies to review before you take the test.

Canceling Scores

If you finish either test and do not feel confident in your potential scores, you have the right to cancel them. You must let your testing proctor know after completing the test that you would like your scores to be canceled.

However, some students end up scoring higher than they expected, so it is advisable not to cancel your scores, because you can't really know how well you did until you see the results. If the results fall short of your expectations, you can use your scores as incentives to discern your shortfalls, consult some of the resources for score improvement mentioned above, and retake the test with better preparation.

Besides, you will not be able to receive a refund for the test if you cancel your scores.

Receiving Scores

Two to eight weeks after taking the SAT or ACT, you will be able to see your scores on the testing websites. It is important to open your scores without expectations, especially on your first round. Practice-test scores are often significantly higher than those from the actual testing situation. Prepare for anything, and do not be upset if your scores do not lie exactly where you hoped they would.

If you would like to see where your scores stand among students that were accepted to the colleges you were applying to, look up the mid 50-percentile test scores for the previously admitted class, which you can find by Google-searching each school's freshman profile. Your goal should be to lie within or above the test-score range of the previously admitted class. If your score is far from the range, I recommend changing your test-preparation strategies and retaking the test to get as close as possible to the range.

However, do not overdo it. Some people are naturally not good test-takers, which no amount of preparation can change. This is why the college admissions process has multiple components, not just test scores.

Sending Scores

Sending my test scores was one of the most confusing processes in my college applications. Counselors and teachers do not adequately explain how it is done or how to choose which scores to send. Different blogs and websites have different opinions on how many scores are too many to send and other issues that could alter your chances of admission.

My advice is to avoid using the free test-score sending service the first time you take the test. It is important to see where your score stands in relation to those of other students, especially if you will be retaking the exam and if the score you receive is something you want to send to admissions offices.

Super-scoring

Super-scoring is the act of combining all or some of an applicant's test sub-scores to make the best possible composite score. Most colleges will mention on their admissions website whether or not they super-score; otherwise, you can e-mail the admissions office to ask them.

If a school does use super-scoring, I suggest you send the scores that would make the highest composite. I took the ACT four times, but sent the two scores that made the highest super-score. This allowed me to save money as well.

Keeping Track of Which Schools Receive Which Test Scores

It is a good idea to keep track of your test-score payments with printouts and screenshots of them, as well as taking screenshots of the test-score receipt confirmation pages in case some of your choice schools do not receive your scores. I also kept a notebook and wrote down my test dates, the names of the schools I sent the scores to, and the dates I sent them.

Each school you apply to should send you log-on information for its online portal, which will show the components of your application they have and have not received. (Be aware that some schools only show certain information and may not display which test dates they have received from you.)

Double-check with each individual college everything you are sending to it. I found out after the submission deadline that a school did not receive one of the three test scores I had sent them, so I had to set up phone calls with the testing center and the admissions office to work out the issue, and ended up having to pay for the test scores to be resent. Make sure an easily avoidable inconvenience with your test scores does not happen to you.

Add Up the Fees

Sending test scores to colleges can get expensive. If you are on a budget, I suggest sending multiple scores to the schools that interest you the most and sending only one score to your "safety" schools (those with acceptance rates higher than 60%, that you stand a good chance of getting in).

Other Tests

SAT Subject Tests

What are they? SAT Subject Tests, a.k.a. SAT IIs, are admissions exams focused on a specific subject of your choice. They highlight your strengths and show your abilities in specific academic fields. Some schools require students to submit these tests; others may recommend them for certain majors, or not require them at all. An advantage of the Subject Tests is: you can take up to three on one date. Most schools that require these tests require two scores to be sent to them, but if you decide to take three at once, you can choose your top scores from the bunch.

Which schools require them? Many highly selective and prestigious schools may require SAT Subject Test scores along with SAT scores. (A list of the schools that use these tests can be found on the College Board website, collegeboard.org.) Many students have never heard of these tests and find out that their schools need their scores when it is too late. So visit each school's admissions website to look at their testing requirements, because they vary from school to school.

Which should you take? When choosing which Subject Tests to take, you need to consider your academic strengths and the application requirements of your choice colleges. Of course, if their admissions offices require certain exams, then you will be taking those. However, if they leave the choice up to you, you must reflect on your academic history. If you are a strong English student, consider taking the Subject Test in English. If you earned a low grade in a math class but you believe you know the material, take a Mathematics Subject Test to show admissions officers your true abilities.

When should you take them? When deciding to take subject tests, it is important to think ahead. The College Board recommends that students take the exams the spring after they complete the suggested courses, when the information is fresh in your mind and you can perform at your best abilities. (Recommended courses are listed on the College Board website, collegeboard.org.) Most of these tests are taken in the spring of students' sophomore and junior years.

How do you register? Registering for the subject tests is very similar to registering for the SAT: through the College Board website (collegeboard.org). You must pay for each exam you are taking on that testing date, unless you have an exam fee waiver.

How are they scored? Subject Tests are scored on a scale of 200-800. Foreign language exams also report a listening section sub-score of 20-80.

AP Exams

Advanced Placement (AP) Examinations are designed to measure the knowledge students gained in their AP courses. These tests are given in May each year through the College Board and are scored on a scale of 1-5:

5 – Extremely well qualified

4 – Well qualified

3 – Qualified

2 – Possibly qualified

1 – No recommendation

Students who score high enough on these exams (usually 3, 4 or 5) may become eligible for one or two college credits per exam, depending on their chosen school's test-score requirements.

AP exams usually do not reach colleges until after a student decides to enroll—in other words, they are not part of your admissions process. However, some students do choose to send these scores to colleges when applying, if they took AP exams in any of their underclassman years. High scores of 4 or 5 are impressive and offer another resource for admissions officers to use when evaluating your academic performance. (Deciding not to send these scores will not hurt your admissions chances unless a college specifies that requirement on its admissions website.)

Before I applied to college, I had taken only two AP exams (AP United States History and AP Psychology, with respective scores of 3 and 4). I did not send these scores to my choice schools to be considered for admission, because additional fees would have incurred, and I did not see these scores as vital components of my application.

IB Exams

The International Baccalaureate (IB) program is similar to the AP program, except that IB is a two-year program with exams scored on a scale of 1-7. Information about these courses and exams can be found on the IB website, ibo.org.

CHAPTER 3

COLLEGE SEARCH

When you first start thinking of colleges during your underclassman years of high school, you may find that your list is full of Ivy League and other "brand name" schools. Many students find themselves starting at this point, which is okay at first.

However, you must take the searching process a step further to discover the schools that are the right match for you academically and socially. After doing a little research, you may find that you have an entirely different opinion about the schools on your first college list. Take your time, and you will begin to find schools that appear to have the right environment for you, based on whether they fit you academically (GPA and test scores), socially, and personally. The schools on this list should also fit your future career goals and make you feel at home on their campuses.

Determining Your Ideal School

In the beginning stages of your college search, identify the physical, environmental, social, academic and extracurricular characteristics you want to see in your future college or university. Here are a few to help you brainstorm:

Location and Weather: Do you want your campus to be a two-hour drive away from home, or a five-hour flight across the country? Have you lived in the snow all your life and want to go to a school near the beach for a change, or vice versa?

Surrounding Community: Would you like your school to be placed within the downtown of a bustling city, in a quieter college town, or in the countryside?

The Type of School: There are many different "types" of colleges and universities, including: liberal arts, Ivy League, public state colleges and universities, private colleges and universities, religiously affiliated schools, art schools, technical/engineering schools, junior colleges, etc.

Campus Atmosphere: Consider how many students you want to be around. A campus with 5,000 undergraduates has a completely different vibe than a campus with 25,000. Also find out how diverse the student body is by learning about the different cultural backgrounds represented on campus.

Learn about student life: Do students cheer on the sports teams, go to parties, or participate in community ser-vice projects? Talk to students and alumni at your choice schools to learn what kinds of activities mean the most to the student body.

Academics: Find out whether your choice schools offer the major(s) and minor(s) you can see yourself potentially studying. Class sizes and levels of student interaction with professors are other considerations. Some students also consider how early they can get into their major, because some public state universities only allow this come junior year. Finally, learn about whether the classroom holds a collaborative or competitive environment. Are students helping each other to succeed, or is everyone more self-sufficient?

Extracurriculars: Do you play a sport? Are you dying to be the host of a college radio station? Have you been in robotics all of high school and want to continue it in college? See what kinds of programs your school offers for your outside-of-the-classroom interests.

Campus Visit: Visiting a campus can give you a first-hand look at the campus facilities, libraries, and classrooms. Sometimes you do not know what you want in a school until you visit a couple of them. I will expand on the details of college visits later in this chapter.

Six Steps to Developing Your College List

1. **Brainstorm** what you want in a college, write a description of your ideal college, and write down 20 schools you might be interested in learning more about. Google-searching "Top Schools for _____ undergraduate majors" can give you a quick list of many schools that specialize in your desired field(s) of study.

2. **Research** the colleges you wrote down. This need not be done in one day—take your time to learn about each school and refer to your description of your ideal col-

lege along the way. My favorite websites to use include: bigfuture.collegeboard.org and parchment.com.

3. **Cross out** the schools that you do not picture yourself attending, and that are missing many characteristics from your ideal college description. Narrow the list down to about 10 schools.

4. **Determine** your chances of getting into the schools on your list. Google the school's "freshman profile" from the previous admissions year. This will show the average GPA, test scores, and other useful information, such as the number of AP courses the students took in high school.

5. **Arrange** your college list into "Reach," "Range" and "Good Chance / Safety" categories:

   • **"Reach"** schools have acceptance rates under 30% and have many students with higher high-school GPAs and test scores than yourself.

   • **"Range"** schools have acceptance rates from 50%-60% and have many students whose high-school GPAs and test scores fall in line with yours.

   • **"Good Chance / Safety"** schools have acceptance rates higher than 60% and have many students whose high-school GPAs and test scores fall on a par with or below yours.

6. **Choose** about 4-10 schools you wish to apply to in the fall of your senior year. Many students become conflicted on how many colleges they should apply to. My ad-

vice is to apply to 2 "Reach" schools, 3 "Range" schools, and 1-2 "Good Chance / Safety" schools. After you fit schools into those three categories, feel free to add a couple more if you are really considering them as options. Do not apply to schools simply to see if you can get in. Ask yourself, "If I am admitted, would I seriously consider going here?" I see no reason for a student to apply to 15 or more schools, other than not having done their research.

College Visits

Once you finish your tentative college list, it is time to think about visiting some or all of these schools. While it isn't feasible for everyone's family to travel to see colleges, it is something to consider to help you decide on the right place for you.

Choosing When to Visit

I believe the best time to visit schools is around your junior year. College visits take a lot of planning, so if you are a sophomore, it would be wise to start talking to your parents about going to see some of the schools on your list.

Try to plan the visits around a school break. Summertime is most convenient for most families; however, you must remember that, during summer, winter and spring breaks, most students are not on the campus and the admissions office may be closed. If students are not there, you may not get the full experience of the campus vibe and student population.

If you have friends or older siblings who are visiting colleges, see if you can tag along with them. Even if you are not considering the schools they are visiting, you will still learn a lot about the type of institution, which can help you when comparing similar schools.

Some students also may choose to hold off on their college visits until after they are admitted. While this does not help them choose which schools to apply to, the student saves time and money by traveling only to the schools they are considering attending. If you choose to wait until you receive admission, make sure you allow yourself enough time to complete your visits before the college's enrollment and housing deadlines.

Choosing Which Schools to Visit

My college list contained schools from all around the country. I was not able to visit all of them because of time, money and distance. However, there are a few guidelines to think about when deciding which schools to go see.

The easiest schools to visit will be within convenient driving range of where you live. Those are easy to plan for, and will only take a day to drive down, visit, and return home. On the contrary, if your #1 school is across the country, you will have to factor in airline tickets, hotels, and other travel plans into your visit.

If you are limited on the number of schools you can travel to, I suggest you visit one of each "type" of school you are considering. For example, I had four large public universities on my initial college list. I visited one and realized I did not like the atmosphere of 30,000 undergraduate students placed in a small town (however, some people may love this!). By visiting the types of schools you are applying to, you can eliminate or choose to keep schools that are similar on your college list. Prioritize your college visits by the schools that interest you the most. In the end, it is all about finding your perfect campus environment.

Another visiting option available at many campuses are overnight programs. The admissions office or campus organizations may sponsor days where perspective students can come and stay on campus. High-school students are usually partnered with current students who will house them and show them the ins and outs of campus life. Depending on the school, these programs may be offered for free.

How to Schedule Your Visit

Visit the admissions website of each respective school and find the page for campus tours. Almost every school has an online calendar where you can sign up for admissions sessions and campus tours. These usually fill up fast, so schedule them ahead of time.

Also, think about the time for which you are scheduling your tour. A morning session will require you to wake up early, and the campus may not yet be active at the time of your arrival, but will be cooler to walk through in the morning if it's summertime. An afternoon session will allow you to see the campus in full swing, but in the summer it will be very hot walking through the campus, particularly if it is a school located in a warm environment.

What Happens on the Visit

Admissions Session: I found the admissions sessions to be most valuable when visiting schools because, during the sessions, an admissions officer lays out the guidelines of what they seek in a student. They also are a great resource for asking specific questions about your personal application.

Campus Tour: A current student will tour you around campus and inside buildings and classrooms while answering your questions about campus life and student activities. If you are visiting a school during the summer, make sure you are hydrated and wearing walking shoes and breathable clothing, because it will be H-O-T! During your campus tour you may also have an opportunity to go see the dorms. Usually they can take you through only one dorm facility, but that one is usually the nicest on campus.

Personal Exploration of the Campus

There are many things I suggest students check out while on campus that they may not see on the tour. These include:

The Admissions Office: I highly suggest visiting the admissions office, because many times they have a place for students to check in so they know you came to visit campus, and they will sometimes let you talk to an admissions rep without appointment! Take note that the admissions office is usually in a different location than the campus welcome center (where you go for your campus tour). Also, when you schedule your campus tour, see if they offer on-campus interviews on the day you will be visiting.

Campus Dining: Try to eat lunch at a popular dining spot on campus. Sometimes the campus welcome center will have free meal vouchers enabling guests to eat in the dining hall.

Surrounding Area: You will most likely leave campus at some point during your undergraduate years, so take a drive around the surrounding neighborhood and city to see if this is the type of town you would want to live near for four years. Colleges often offer guided bus tours of their cities and towns.

If You Can't Visit Any Schools...

Sometimes it is not feasible for a student to visit any schools, near or far. When this is the case, I recommend looking on the school website for an online virtual tour. Also, on YouTube many students post campus tours of their schools, as well as dorm-room tours. You can also check out campus tour videos on my website, joiwade.com. In today's digital age, there are many ways to learn about a school if you are unable to visit it in person.

CHAPTER 4

RELATIONSHIPS WITH COLLEGES

One of the most important, yet most overlooked, steps in the college admissions process is keeping consistent contact with admissions officers. When it comes to highly competitive schools, to have the best chance possible of gaining admission and scholarships, one must demonstrate interest and go beyond merely filling out the application. There are many things students can do to demonstrate their interest in a school.

College Admissions Reps

The first thing to understand is how your application is reviewed after pressing the 'Submit' button. Your application is reviewed on many tiers. First, your local admissions representatives will read the applications for those students in their region or state. Then, if they believe you have a strong application, they will put you through to the next reviewer and vouch for you in the subsequent steps of the decision process. Other processes may include a committee decision, splitting the applicants by major, admissions "hooks" (minority, first generation, legacy, etc.), and finally reaching the dean of admissions for approval.

It is important to know the admissions process so you know which people in it you need to spend the most time trying to connect with. I believe the most important person from the applicant's perspective is not the dean of admissions, but the local admissions representatives. They read your application first; if it does not pass through them, you lose your admission chances. These people will be the most easily accessible by e-mail and in person. They are easy to develop a relationship with, as they often conduct the college visits to cities and local schools in your area. So use them as a resource for information and assistance, just as you would with your high school guidance counselor. If you make your name known to these admissions officers when your name comes up in their piles of applicants, they will be able to associate a face to the application, which could potentially have a positive effect on your admissions possibilities.

Most college and university admissions websites will have a link through which you can find your local admissions rep and that person's contact information. I suggest making an initial contact through e-mail, telling them who you are, what major interests you, and what high school you attend. Then ask them if they will be in your area anytime soon. After you send this initial e-mail—preferably in your sophomore or junior year—follow up with this contact only to ask any questions you have about the admissions process; you do not want to spam your admissions officers so much they get annoyed with you.

Balance your contact with your admissions officers so that you become a memorable student, but are not annoying them with tons of e-mails.

Meeting in Person

Colleges host on- and off-campus events in which students meet representatives from those schools. These include perspective student events, college fairs, and even visits to your high school. Stay on top of the dates and locations of these events, as they are a great time to meet admissions officers, current students or graduates and ask them questions. Ask your guidance counselor about colleges that will be sending representatives to your school or your area.

Other Ways to Demonstrate Interest in a School

You can also continue to show your interest in a particular college or university by:

- Joining the mailing list on the school website

- Scheduling an on-campus or off-campus interview

- Following your school's admissions office on social media

- Checking in at the admissions office during your campus visit

- Participating in an optional admissions interview

- Attending a summer program at that school

CHAPTER 5

PREPARING FOR APPLICATIONS

Before you begin your applications you must begin to organize the process in your mind to help you save time and energy building your perfect portfolio about yourself. This includes making an activities resume, finding recommenders, and thinking ahead about your essays.

Activities Resume

One of the resources I used the most throughout my application process was my activities resume. During my sophomore year, I made a document on which I listed all of my extracurricular pursuits: sports, clubs, community service, awards, etc. I continued to add items during my junior year. The summer before my senior year, I took this list and transformed it into a resume. I then printed out multiple copies to keep in my book bag, my room, and anywhere else I would work on college applications.

You probably won't submit your activities resume to any colleges. This is mainly a resource for you to consult as you complete college applications. Some scholarships may require you to submit a resume, however—and your activities resume will come in handy for that. With this convenient document, you won't have to think back to what you did spring semester freshman year, because it is already written down in front of you.

Items to include on your resume: clubs, sports, community service, hobbies, summer experiences, special skills and talents, languages you speak, awards and recognitions, study abroad experiences, and any other unique activities and organizations you are involved in inside or outside of school.

Your activities resume will also help you reach an important goal: to give each of your college applications an overlying theme. For instance, I knew I wanted to apply to journalism schools, and I wanted my application to show my passion for communication and media. So I made sure to put my participation in the school newspaper, yearbook, TV station and other related organizations high on my activities list, because they were the most relevant to the type of school I was applying for. I omitted activities that were irrelevant to my application theme, or that I had partici-pated in for less than one year. See **Appendix B** to read a copy of my resume.

Recommendation Letters

'Do I Get to Read My Letters?'

The Common Application has an online form that requires you to sign off, saying you will not read the recommendations you are submitting. This is called waiving your right to view your recommendation letters. By not reading them, it adds validity to the words your teacher, counselor or other submitter is saying. You also have the option not to sign off.

How Many Letters to Submit

If you are using the Common Application, your guidance counselor is already prompted to submit a recommendation and school report for you. This does *not* count toward the number of recommendations your colleges will require of you. Go on *each* school's website and look up its specific application requirements to see how many recommendation letters are needed. The more selective schools may require two recommendation letters.

Many schools allow additional recommendation letters as well. You should submit additional letters only if you believe that it is vital to your application and that the letter shows the admissions office a new side not revealed in your essays, activities and other materials.

Whom to Ask for Letters

* **Your guidance counselor from your current high school** (does not count toward the number of required recommendation letters).

* **A teacher who taught you in a core major subject during your junior year.** Choose one related to your major—i.e., a math teacher for engineering, a science teacher for biochemistry, an English or history teacher for humanities. That way, admissions officers can hear from someone who has taught you recently in a field re-

lated to your intended major—preferably in an AP or Honors class, to demonstrate your readiness for college-level work in that field.

If you changed high schools in your junior or senior year, consider asking for letters from the guidance counselor or a teacher at your previous high school.

After you receive these fundamental recommendation letters, it is time to think about whom you will ask for the other required or additional recommendations you will submit. Those options include:

* **A teacher in a *different* subject** who knows you well and will speak from a different perspective than the first teacher.

>Remember, you do not need perfect grades in the class of the teacher you ask. If you worked hard to get a B in the course and the teacher saw improvement over time, this could look better on your application than a recommendation coming from a teacher who taught a course you easily slid through with an A+.

* **An advisor in an extracurricular activity** you have been heavily involved in (sports, clubs, outside-of-school pursuits, etc.).

Whom *Not* to Ask for Letters

* Family members

* People you have known for a short time

* A teacher you are not fond of

When to Ask and How Many to Ask For

Start thinking early about whom you want to ask for recommendation letters—preferably during the spring of your junior year. I suggest asking at least three people for recommendations outside of your guidance counselor. You may not end up using them all on your college applications, but you will definitely want choices when the time comes. Having extra letters ready will also make the scholarship application process easier, as colleges often require more than one recommendation letter.

Planning Your Letter

Before you ask your teachers and advisors, it is important to plan out what you want your letters to reveal about you. You should not leave it solely in the recommender's hands to decide what to write about you. Many students will just ask for a recommendation and assume that their teacher or guidance counselor will write what they want them to. To ensure that your recommendations are strong and unique, make an outline of the qualities, strengths and achievements you want highlighted in your letter and give it to each teacher to use as a guide to writing the letter.

This is especially important because you may already emphasize certain qualities or facts about yourself in your application essay. It would not make sense for your teacher to write about the same exact situation (that could also raise suspicion in the admission officer's mind that you may have fabricated the letter). You need letters that will bring new information about you and your strengths to the table and promote you in a fresh way.

In addition to your outline, you should consider giving your teacher a copy of your activities resume as well. (Personally, I did not give some of my recommendation writers the resume, because I did not want them to write a list of activities that were already written on my application.) Choose which resources you want them to use to aid them in their writing, that would present your strengths most effectively from a vantage point other than yours.

Brainstorming Essay Ideas

The summer before senior year is the perfect time to think about your Common Application essay idea. The Common Application website lists the five prompts from which you will have to choose. The prompts are made available each summer before the Common Application portal opens.

While it is tempting to look at the prompts right away, I suggest first brainstorming topics you would like to write about. Then, once you settle on an idea, find a way to fit that into a prompt.

When brainstorming, write down all of your ideas, even the ones you may not think you will use. Try to stick to anecdotes that are focused on one event, rather than trying to talk about your whole life, all of your extracurriculars, or other broad subjects.

I will talk more about the college essay in **Chapter 7.**

Admissions Hooks and Special Circumstances

In college admissions, schools look out for special characteristics to increase school diversity. Admissions hooks could improve your chances of being admitted or enhance your application, so if you fall under any of these categories, list them on your application:

First Generation: First-generation students' parents or guardians have not received a four-year bachelors degree. In other words, these students are the first in their family to attend college.

Minority: Minority students have been historically underrepresented in school populations. For example, at a historically black college or university (HBCU), African-American students are not in the minority, so minority status as an African-American would not be as helpful in admissions. At predominately white institutions (PWIs), minority students almost always include those from black and Latino backgrounds. However, many college admissions officers do not count those from Asian backgrounds in their minority applications if that ethnicity is thoroughly represented.

Legacy: A legacy student's parents, grandparents and/or siblings have attended that school before them.

Special Talents: Special talents can include sports or the arts. Many recruiters for colleges and universities look in advance for these talents in prospective students well before their senior year and use those criteria to attract students to their schools. So, if you have a special talent, develop it well in your high-school years and make sure your top-choice schools are aware of it well before the admissions process. If you are interested in playing a sport in college, make sure you complete all of the NCAA requirements early on in your high-school career so schools can start looking at you. If you are an artist, build your portfolio, and exhibit your work as much as you can. If you are an actor, dancer or musician, give enough performances and recitals to note proudly on your activities resume.

National Merit Scholar, Perfect Test Scores, and More: If you receive exceptional standardized test scores, you could receive additional attention or scholarships from schools. However, bear in mind that students with perfect test scores can be rejected from the top schools if the remainders of their applications are not up to par academically.

CHAPTER 6

APPLICATION TIME

Going into your senior year of high school means you have a long road of college visits, applications, essays, anticipations, and decisions ahead of you.

Types of Applications

Common Application: The Common Application website has partnered with colleges to enable students to apply to multiple schools using one application and one main essay. Many students will complete a large portion of their college applications on this site. Most schools you will be applying to may be partnered with the Common Application; thus you will fill out one application to send to every school. Schools may also require supplemental information, essays, or short answers, which will be listed right on the application. Websites similar to the Common Application include the Universal College Application and the Common Black College Application.

Institutional Applications: Many public universities will have their own applications separate from the Common Application. Sometimes you can choose between a school's particular application and the Common Application. Using one instead of the other does not increase your admission chances. In fact, school-specific applications often ask questions very similar to those on the Common Application, and will also have a spot for your college essay, which usually has different prompt options than those in the Common Application.

When to Apply

Early Decision: Early Decision applications are a binding agreement that, if you are admitted to the school, you agree to enroll there. You are allowed to apply Early Decision to only one school. These applications are due around November of your senior year, and students usually hear back around mid December. Many students stray away from Early Decision applications, because they are often not able to see financial aid before making their decision. However, if you are certain that a particular school is your top choice and you want to hear back sooner than the spring, Early Decision is a good option.

Early Action: Early Action applications are similar to Early Decision, but are not binding. Once you receive your Early Action admissions decision, you can still decide to enroll somewhere else.

Restrictive Early Action: A Restrictive Early Action application requires you to sign an agreement that you will apply Early Action to only one school.

Regular Decision: Regular Decision is the normal process by which students apply to college, with no binding agreements or early deadlines. Regular Decision deadlines usually occur around January. When applying Regular Decision, admissions decisions are usually released in the spring. Most students fall into the Regular Decision pool because it allows them more time to perfect their applications and make the right college choice. Some schools may offer only this choice for application.

Rolling Admission: In Rolling Admission applications, students receive their admissions decisions as soon as the admissions office is finished reading their application materials. Many public and smaller universities offer this type of admission process.

Application Components

Personal Information: This component of the application will ask for the easy information: your name, address, phone number, e-mail address, and possibly your Social Security number. I recommend you set up a special e-mail address for all of your college information, because you will be receiving many e-mails from perspective schools. The e-mail should be simple and should include your first and last name; it should not be the embarrassing e-mail address you created in middle school.

Transcript: Your high-school transcript is your record of your academic performance from your freshman year to the end of your junior year. Many high schools and colleges send and accept transcripts electronically. Your high-school counselor should explain which method to use when sending your transcripts to each school you are applying to. Make sure you receive confirmation that each school received this part of your application.

Mid-Year and Final Grades: After you submit your application, colleges like to see the grades you are earning during your senior year. Depending on the school, your guidance counselor may be required to submit your updated grades through the Common Application, or you may have to self-report them on an online form.

Extracurriculars: This is where you will list and explain all of the clubs, sports, and activities you have participated in throughout high school. List them in the order of their importance to you, from most important at the top to least important at the bottom. Do not be afraid to omit a club if you were not heavily involved in it; you do not have to fill every single slot of activities simply to impress an admissions officer. It actually looks better when you have fewer activities you have participated in for multiple years, from which you have gained leadership positions, awards, or other accolades.

Test Scores: For your choice schools to receive your standardized test scores, you must manually send them via the College Board or ACT website. Unless you have score report fee waivers, you will have to pay for each score you send to your schools. Make sure you send these scores early, because they can take a few weeks to be processed into the school's system.

Essays and Supplements: If you are using the Common Application, you will have to complete the Common Application essay only once. This will be sent to every college, unless you revise your essay, or customize it according to a particular school's requirements, before sending it to other schools. Colleges may re-quire you to write additional essays or write short answers to questions, so treat these with the same level, or even a higher level, of importance as your Common Application essay.

Teacher, Counselor, and Additional Recommenda-tions: Recommendation letters enable an admissions offi-cer to learn about you from the perspective of an adult or mentor in your life. These recommendations should reveal information about your academic performance and per-sonal qualities. They should not be a copy-and-paste of your activities resume or application essay. These letters should reveal new information about you that has not al-ready been stated in other places in your application.

Admissions Interviews

Many highly selective schools offer, or even require, ad-missions interviews. They can be conducted in person, over the phone, or via a video chat application such as Skype, FaceTime or Google Hangouts. If you live near the school or are visiting, you could be invited to interview on campus. If you live a distance away, the school may find a nearby alumnus or alumna to conduct the interview in a public place, such as a coffee shop or a library conference room.

Admissions interviews add another level of depth to your application, and I suggest checking to see if your top school choice offers them. They rarely affect your application negatively, because they are a way for the admissions office to get to know you on a more personal level.

Tips for Interviews

1. Before the interview, write down five reasons why you want to attend this particular school. Try to differentiate among reasons that involve academics, student life, campus qualities, extracurriculars, and career opportunities.

2. Prepare a list of questions to ask the interviewer pertaining to your reasons for wanting to enroll at that school and what the school has to offer, as a way of expressing your genuine interest in the school.

3. Do practice interviews with friends and family, in which you take turns asking your prepared questions, to make yourself more comfortable with the interview process before the big event.

4. Dress professionally to make a great first impression on the interviewer. Arrive at least 15 minutes before your scheduled interview time so you can go over your interview notes and questions, make a bathroom stop, comb your hair, have a drink of water, etc.

5. Bring along a copy of your activities resume as a guide for conversation. Also, have a copy on hand to give to your interviewer if appropriate.

6. Greet the interviewer with a smile, good eye contact, and a firm but not overly hard handshake. Make your first impression warm and genuine, not forced and politician-like.

7. Engage in a friendly conversation with the interviewer to establish a good rapport with that person, as opposed to trying to memorize a script beforehand.

8. Answer the interviewer's questions directly, and keep your answers fairly short and to the point. Don't talk too long or go off on tangents. Show your genuine interest in the school in your answers, but don't appear too eager or desperate.

9. Ask questions that demonstrate your curiosity about the school and its academic, social and extracurricular offerings, and that are pertinent to your interests and goals, but don't be too self-serving.

10. Avoid fidgeting, squirming, shifting your weight, making annoying facial expressions, or displaying any other physical signs of nervous tension. If you feel nervous before your interview, arrive early and take a few deep breaths before you go in.

11. Above all, be yourself. Let the real you shine through, rather than answer the interviewer's questions the way you think that person wants you to. Don't be afraid to laugh and enjoy the interview!

12. After the interview, be sure to get the contact information of the interviewer. In a timely manner, send that person a thank-you card by regular mail (not e-mail) to

make a more lasting impression.

In the back of this book are common questions asked in admissions interviews and suggestions on how to answer them.

Tryouts and Auditions

If you wish to attend a particular school for its sports or arts program, you may be required to try out or audition for the program, in addition to completing your application. Early in your process, talk to an admissions counselor, coach, or department head about how to set up your audition. Figure out if you have to travel to campus, create a video audition, or submit a portfolio of your work. Make sure that you complete all of your submissions on time and that they reach the school departments in charge of the programs you are applying to.

CHAPTER 7

ESSAYS & SUPPLEMENTS

Every year, students struggle to compose the perfect admissions essay to impress their dream school. No matter how simple or complex the prompt may be, there are some simple steps you can take to bring your college essay to the next level.

10 Tips About College Application Essays

1. Start early. You do not want to write your college essay the night before it is due. I started my essay process the summer before my senior year and completed a rough draft before I started school that fall. If you can get ahead on your essay, you are eliminating one of the hardest parts of the process.

2. Think small. Do not try to write about every little detail in your life. This will lead to an unfocused, confusing essay. Think of anecdotes from important milestone events in your life. These should be unique to you—if you think anyone else could have written something similar to your essay, it is time to brainstorm a new idea.

3. Avoid clichés and common topics. While some topics like sports, a death in the family, and how your bar mitzvah was a transition into adulthood may be important to you, admissions officers have seen these way too many times. You wan to make a specialized essay that is one-of-a-kind and one that only you could write.

4. Outline three different essays. Take a look at your essay prompts and see which one your ideas may fit into the best. Once you figure this out, it is time to start planning your essay. Sometimes a good idea may not turn into the best essay. Take your top three essay topics and make an informal outline for each. Consider making one for different Common Application prompts as well, because you may end up with a great essay you did not consider initially.

5. Write your rough draft. Remember, this essay is not like the papers you write for your English class.

- *Make your essay conversational, so it will reveal your voice and personality.* Don't make it overly academic in tone and style.

- *Show, don't tell.* Instead of writing about how serious you are about schoolwork, tell a story of, for instance, a time you spent four hours studying for the hardest exam in your life, and how your hard work paid off in the end, or something similar. Emphasize the *results* of your efforts.

- *Consider your audience.* A college admissions officer who does not know you personally will be reading this. So make sure you do not leave out details your friends and family already know.

- *While writing, think about what emotions you want to evoke from your audience.* Choose your words carefully to reflect the tone of the story.

6. Show your draft to at least three people for feedback. I am a very self-sufficient person, and I wanted to handle most of the application process myself. However, it is crucial to show your essay to a teacher, a guidance counselor, a parent, or a friend. These people can tell you if there are grammar mistakes, if they can hear your voice in the essay, or if they have seen similar college essays before. Once you receive all of your feedback, look over the suggestions and make the changes to your liking.

7. Rewrite and edit your draft. After writing, it is easy to believe you have a finished product, but you should take the time to edit your writing several times to ensure that your essay is the best it can be. Edit it with a fresh mind. College essays are one of the only times an admissions officer can see your writing talents and hear what you have to say. You do not want to restrict that because of simple grammatical errors.

8. Rewrite and edit some more. This essay is very important and it can determine the next four years of your life. It can affect your college acceptance and even your scholarship opportunities. This is why your application essay must be of the best quality you can produce.

9. Take a break. Do not submit your essay as soon as you think you are done. If you are finishing up a few weeks ahead of deadlines, take a week off and do not read your essay at all. After the break, come back with fresh eyes and see if there are any errors you missed or changes you need to make. Read your essay aloud, and let someone read it to you so you can catch awkward sentences and phrases more keenly.

10. Polish your final copy. Do not become too tedious with your essay. At some point you will have to decide to stop the writing process and print out a final copy. Show your final copy to someone to read over and make comments on the printout.

11. Submit your final essay to the Common Application. Once you have done all you can do to make your essay your best-written work, it is time to submit it to the Common Application. Note that once you send it to a college, you cannot make any changes. However, you can make edits, or completely change your prompt and essay, before sending it to other schools.

Recycling your Essays

Many times college and scholarship applications will have similar essay questions. You do not have to write a new essay each time if your original essay illustrates what the prompt is asking for. Make sure you make any additions, omissions, and changes to your essay to make it fit the new prompt before submitting.

Supplements

In the Common Application, colleges have the option to ask for additional essays or short answers. Many students see these add-ons as less important than other parts of their application such as their main essays. However, many schools weigh their supplements more heavily than those other components. So use the above steps you followed for your main essay to write quality supplements.

Common College Supplement Questions:

Why do you want to attend this college?

This essay is a way for the admissions office to see whether you have actually done your research on the school. Many students are very vague when completing this supplement question, because they know few details about the institution. To go into this supplement equipped for success, spend some time looking through the school's website. Learn about special opportunities available for students in your major. Inform yourself on notable faculty and research opportunities that undergraduates can get involved in. Also, think about what you want to partake in outside of the class, too, by reading up on the student organizations available on campus. Avoid general things like talking about the city the school is placed in. The admissions office wants to know specifically why you want to attend that school and how its offerings pertain to your vocational and personal goals and will meet your needs in those areas.

Describe an extracurricular activity you are involved in, and explain why it is important to you.

Choose one activity and recall in detail one of your favorite moments of participation in it. Use that one specific anecdote to illustrate the role you had in that activity. Think about what you want the supplement to reveal about you: leadership, team-playing ability, performance in the face of adversity, or other desirable qualities.

CHAPTER 8

FINANCIAL AID & SCHOLARSHIPS

For some students, getting into college is not important unless they receive the right funds from financial aid and scholarships to attend. With the average cost of attendance for both public and private institutions across the country on the rise, it is important to learn the basics of financial aid and scholarships so attending college can be made more affordable.

Before You Start

Before you begin your financial aid applications, make sure you have your parents' tax information for the previous and current years. Many schools require you to submit tentative information from the previous year much earlier than the current year's tax season. You will also need the Social Security numbers of you and your parents.

Need-based Aid vs. Merit-based Aid

Need-based aid is determined from family financial information provided in the FAFSA and the CSS/Financial Aid PROFILE® (see below), as well as other financial aid forms. Aid can be given in the form of grants, scholarships, and loans.

Merit-based aid, such as the National Merit Scholarships, is money given to students based primarily on their academic achievements. Merit-based aid takes the form of grants that do not have to be paid back to the school or the government.

Need-based Aid

FAFSA. The Free Application for Federal Student Aid (FAFSA) is a form created by the federal government that asks for important financial information about your family. With this information, an expected family contribution (EFC) is calculated. This is how much the FAFSA believes your family can afford to pay for college, based on your family's financial information. Almost all colleges require the FAFSA for financial aid consideration. The FAFSA website is: fafsa.ed.gov/

CSS/Financial Aid PROFILE®. This is another financial aid form created by the College Board. Many private institutions require this form in addition to the FAFSA for financial aid consideration. This form is much more lengthy than the FAFSA and requires more family financial information. The CSS/Financial Aid PROFILE® website is: student.collegeboard.org/css-financial-aid-profile

Tips: Print out hard copies of the applications and fill them out with your parents with pen and paper. Highlight any answers you will need to return to later on. Once you fill out the hard copy, type all of the information into the computer.

Scholarships

I was awarded the following scholarships:

1. University of Southern California: Presidential Scholarship (Half Tuition), and Wallis Annenberg Scholarship ($25,000/year)
2. University of Miami: Hammond Scholarship (Full Tuition)
3. New York University: Martin Luther King, Jr. Scholarship ($45,000/year)
4. Temple University: $18,000/year
5. Howard University: $14,000/year

I was also a finalist for the Tom Joyner Foundation HBCU Full Ride Scholarship.

Institutional Scholarships

Institutional scholarships come directly from the schools that accept you. These usually come along with your acceptance letters, or shortly thereafter. These scholarships are based on your GPA, your test scores, and the overall quality of your application. Other factors include the number of scholarships available, and the availability of funding for these scholarships. Many colleges have early deadlines for their scholarship applications.

I suggest Google-searching "Your College Merit Scholarships." Some schools list preset GPA and test-score requirements that are aided to all students who qualify. Other schools will list different levels of scholarships but will not state test-score cutoffs. Still others will personally invite students to their campus to interview for large half-tuition or full-tuition scholarships.

Outside Resources

Outside organizations and companies award scholarships as well. From amounts of $300 to a full ride, these scholarships attract a large pool of applicants. (I applied to a plethora of these scholarships— both local and national— in high school, but was not awarded any.)

A few large scholarships include the Questbridge, Posse, Tom Joyner Foundation and Coca-Cola scholarships. There are tons of scholarship web resources, including scholarships.com and the "Scholly" Smartphone app (myscholly.com/#scholly). You can also find local scholarships through your high-school guidance counselor.

Narrow your list down to the scholarships that fit you the best. Thousands are open at a time, so prioritize your time to focus on those you have the best chance at winning. Look for scholarships available only to those who live in your state, city, or even school district. They will have a smaller amount of applicants, thereby increasing your chances of receiving them. Also, try to find scholarships that give awards to multiple students.

If you have a special talent in art, film, etc., look for contests that offer monetary prizes. These are offered year-round by many different organizations.

Scholarship Interviews

Scholarship interviews are similar to admissions interviews, except that you are already accepted to the school at the time! Scholarship interviews are a chance for the school or donor to get to know you personally, so they know whom they would be giving their money to. Assets such as your academic performance, GPA, test scores, etc., are the reason they called you to interview, but their decision to give you the money will be based more on your personality and academic goals.

Thoroughly research the scholarship you are interviewing for. I suggest talking to students who currently have the scholarship at the institution and asking them for advice on appropriate interview questions. If an individual donor or organization is awarding your scholarship, it could be helpful to learn about the donor's mission statement and values, to see how compatible they are with your own.

Appealing Financial Aid

If you are accepted to your top school but have not received enough money for you to attend, consider submitting an appeal to your financial aid office. Get your parents to call, e-mail, and write letters to the office to attempt to get more money from them. If you completed scholarship or admissions interviews that went well, try to talk to those people you met about getting more money. Also see if any freshman scholarships still have open applications. Finally, contact the head of your future academic department to see if it can offer you any scholarship money to study your major.

CHAPTER 9

MAKING THE FINAL CHOICE

After months of test-taking, essay-writing, applying, interviewing, and waiting, the time is here—acceptance, deferral, waitlisting, or denial. Go into this phase with an open mind and no expectations, because anything can happen. Do not take any denial decisions personally, and celebrate the acceptances you do receive. In the end, you will end up in the school you are supposed to be in—I promise.

Accepted!?

It does not matter which institution your first college acceptance comes from. That first 'yes' is a feeling of utter happiness and relief.

I received my first acceptance from Temple University in Philadelphia. They have a rolling admissions process, so I did not know the exact date I would be hearing back from them. One day I decided to check the online portal, and there it was—my first college admission offer.

Excitement rushed through my mind, and I tried to envision myself attending there, even though it was not my top-choice school. My parents read the letter aloud proudly and smiled when they saw I had received a scholarship.

When you are accepted to a college or university, make sure you:

1. Share the good news with your friends and family.

2. Read through the admissions packet carefully and complete any instructions given.

3. Review scholarship and financial aid information carefully when available.

4. Try to visit the school if you have not already done so, if it is a serious consideration.

Deferred? Waitlisted? Denied?

Deferral: A deferral occurs when a student applies under one of the early admission applications and, instead of accepting the student, the admissions office puts off its final decision until the Regular Decision pool is evaluated. A school may choose to do this if they want to learn more about the applicant through additional essays, test scores, or mid-year report grades. If you are deferred, you must keep up your academic record, because your school will be watching you closely. Make sure you complete any other application components that may become available after your notification of deferral. If you are curious about why you were deferred, see if your high school guidance counselor can contact the admissions office to learn about your decision and what they are looking for in the rest of your application.

Waitlist: A waitlist decision occurs when Regular Decision applicants are notified of their admission. Waitlisted students are selected as alternates if students who were accepted decline their admissions and space opens up in the freshman class. If you are put on the waitlist, make sure you confirm or deny your spot on that list. Confirm the spot if you definitely still want to attend the school or keep it as an option. Deny the spot if the school is no longer a serious consideration and you want to give another student a chance of getting in.

If you confirm your spot on the waitlist, I recommend sending a letter to your admissions counselor explaining why you should be released from the waitlist and why their school is still a top choice for you. Showing that you are still very interested in enrolling may get you closer to admission. However, many schools encourage students to consider other admissions options if they are waitlisted. Look at the school's waitlist admissions statistics to see how many students they actually take off the list and offer admission to. If the percentage is low, it is best to commit to a different school, especially if the May 1 commitment deadline is nearing.

Denial: We all know what this one is. It is the hardest news to find out that you were not admitted to one of the schools you applied to—especially if it was one of your top choices.

My Experience

I received one deferral, one waitlist, and one denial. Remember, these decisions are not personal—a college can admit only so many students, and they are looking for the best candidates to fit the new freshman class academically and socially.

The first decision letter I received was a deferral from the University of Georgia (UGA). Receiving this right off the bat discouraged me about my entire college process. I began to question whether any other schools would admit me, and I definitely did not see myself earning any scholarships. I asked my high-school guidance counselor to contact my local admissions representative to learn the reasoning behind my deferral. To my surprise, the school had not received my highest test score, so they deferred me because of where my lower scores stood. Thankfully, UGA allows their deferred students to complete the entire Regular Decision application and resubmit for another consideration. I decided to finish the application and send in my updated test scores, and I was admitted with the Regular Decision pool.

I received a waitlist decision from the University of North Carolina at Chapel Hill. When I applied, I knew the competition for out-of-state students was tough, so I was not sure what their admissions decision would be for me. When admissions decisions were released, I had already heard back from seven of the nine schools to which I applied. Because I already had many acceptances under my belt, including some from my top-choice schools, seeing 'waitlist' on my screen did not take as large of a toll on me as my deferral had done. I already knew where I would most likely attend, so I declined the waitlist offer to give another student a shot at admission.

My only denial came from the only Ivy League institution I applied to: the University of Pennsylvania. Penn was one of the first schools I became attached to early on in my college process, so I decided not to remove it from my college list. I applied to Penn's Wharton Business School, even though my passion is in journalism. I believe that revealed me as weak in showing a passion for business. Though I applied to Penn's Marketing and Communications major, I still received a denial from the university.

Factors to Consider in Making Your Final Choice

Once you receive all of your college decisions back, it is time to make a final choice by your commitment deadline. If you applied Early Decision, then you have it easy: the choice is already made! But if you have received multiple offers from equally attractive schools, it is time to sit down and consider all of your options:

1. Money. A key consideration for many families is the cost of college. Your family must decide how much they are willing to pay for college. If your family is not contributing any money to help you with your education, then you must factor in loans, an on-campus job, and savings for yourself. If a school offers you a large amount of scholarship money, it is worth it to take that offer.

2. Your major. Compare each school to see if one is noticeably a better environment for studying your major.

Try to look into the professors and graduates that are in your desired work field. Find out if students easily get internships and jobs in that field at graduation. Also, see how up-to-date the facilities are, and how well the school pays attention to your particular academic goals.

3. Distance from home. Easy as it is to send applications to schools far away from you, now it is time to actually consider how well you can handle living across the country from home. If you find yourself getting homesick easily, it might be wise to choose a school closer to home. If you move farther away, you will not be able to drive home whenever you want, which could mean missing holidays with your family. On the other hand, if you live near your chosen school and want to go out of your comfort zone, you may not be able to escape the bubble of living at home. Therefore, you must decide where your comfort zone lies so you can make the most responsible decision on where to attend college.

4. Student life. Learn more about the types of students that attend your school, and see if you would find yourself comfortable among them. Some schools focus more on their social aspects; others flaunt their students' dedication to academics. Refer back to the qualities you sought in your initial college search to help you decide.

5. Academic life. Make sure you check up on your major's academic requirements. See if they will accept any credits you have received from AP or IB courses or dual enrollment. Look into any general education requirements you will need to fulfill. Considering the future, think about whether you want to go to graduate, medical, law or business school, and research each school's placement percentages. Overall, try to find the best fit for your academic interests.

Once you make your final decision, submit your enrollment deposit, apply for housing, and notify the schools you will not be attending via e-mail or phone. Oh, and do not forget to celebrate the end of the college-admissions road with your friends and family!

Appendix A: My College List

Temple University	*Accepted*
University of Georgia	*Deferred, Accepted*
University of Miami	*Accepted*
Howard University	*Accepted*
University of Southern California	*Accepted, Enrolled*
New York University	*Accepted*
Northwestern University	*Accepted*
UNC Chapel Hill	*Waitlisted*
University of Pennsylvania	*Denied*

Appendix B: My Activities Resume

JOI K. WADE
My Address
Tel: 123-456-7890
E-mail: mycollegeemail@yahoo.com

EDUCATION

My High School Name   2015-Present
High School's Address

Previous High School's Name   2012-2015
High School's Address

Cumulative GPA: 3.90/4.0
Weighted GPA: 5.9/7.0
Class Rank (as of Feb 2016): 22/412

AP Courses by graduation: 6
* AP US History
* AP Calculus AB
* AP Psychology
* AP English Literature
* AP Physics 1
* AP English Language

Honors Courses: 6

TEST SCORES

ACT Exam
* Composite: 31
* English: 32/36

- Reading: 34/36

EXTRACURRICULARS

- Reporter and Photographer for school newspaper, *The Beacon*
- Director and Co-Anchor, Morning Announcements
- Photography Club, Founder and Club President
- Video Production Club:
  - Attendee and contest participant, Student Television Network (STN) Convention Orlando, Florida
  - Best Cinematography Award at Spring Shorts Film Festival
  - Assistant Editor of Photography, Yearbook

WORK EXPERIENCE

Company Name   Summer 2013-Present
- I am in charge of web design, social media, and merchandising.

Company Name   Summer 2014-Summer 2015
- Contracted Journalist for online and print fashion and web personality magazine.

SPECIAL EDUCATIONAL EXPERIENCES

College Summer Program: Journalism Concentration   July 12-25, 2015
- Spent 30 hours of instruction learning skills in journalism and public relations.

OTHER INTERESTS

YouTube
- Since middle school I have produced and starred in videos dealing with fashion and beauty on my own YouTube channel, MissJoi100, where I have approximately 10,000 subscribers and counting.

Travel
- I have been fortunate enough to experience cultures from a wide variety of countries. Those include: England, France, Italy, Jamaica, and the Bahamas, as well as many domestic travels.

Appendix C: My Common Application Essay

Snowy Decisions

In a swarm of 2,000 high-school students it can be hard to find the courage to speak out against the crowd. Many times, students have wonderful opinions and suggestions but are just too afraid of talking to someone important who can catalyze that change. One day, during my junior year, I decided to cross the threshold of uncertainty. That day was when I found my voice.

As a student from the northeast region, my favorite part of the winter is snow-caused school cancellations. The feeling of being able to hit the snooze button for a few extra hours is quite exemplary. However, these random delays usually result in the utilization of a scheduled snow make-up day later in the school year. When that occurs, I usually give these days no second thought; however, one Friday evening I found myself conflicted and upset when my school board announced that Martin Luther King, Jr. Day, a federal holiday, would be used as a makeup a day due to previous weather.

Upon the district's decision, I instantly gravitated to my family for insight on whether or not I, an African-American student in a predominantly white school, should be required to attend. Personally, I have used the holiday in the past to reflect and spark up conversation on civil rights and other issues with those around me. It did not feel morally correct for me, or any other student who wished to do the same, to attend school. The reactions of my peers on social media revealed to me that I was not in the minority on this opinion.

The school I attended at the time, Dallastown Area High School, has an African-American population of less than 5% and, in addition, no adults of color are a part of the district administration or teaching staff. So naturally, I was not surprised that they had made this call; it had been done years before. However, I noticed that no one was protesting their emotions on why dismissing the holiday was wrong. I viewed this as an opportunity to take action. My community needed a voice.

That Friday, I drafted a thorough letter of enlightenment for the district superintendent expressing the thoughts and feelings of those offended by the mandatory snow makeup day. It included historical and contextual details about Dr. King himself and the importance of observing the holiday. Weaved inside the argument were teacher activities to use inside the classroom, just in case we still were called into the school on the upcoming Monday.

Not only did I send this to the superintendent, I also shared my letter with my peers through my Twitter account. The magic of social media allowed over 6,000 students, parents, and surrounding schools to see what was taking place. The reactions were all supportive, positive, and encouraging. All that remained was to hear back from the man in charge.

When I received a response, the principal and superintendent concluded that it was too late to withdraw the decision. However, they ensured that during the district calendar planning for the upcoming year and every year to follow, Martin Luther King Day would be far from consideration for a snow makeup day.

In the weeks following, parents, teachers, and students applauded me for my initiative. I discussed the issue in person with the principal. I was invited to help lead a diversity awareness group at my school.

All in all, I realized that words are powerful and that sometimes you have to take action, even when those around you may not.

Appendix D: My USC Writing Supplement

Prompt: Describe the extracurricular activity that you are involved in that means the most to you.

At the age of 17, I've spoken to more than 350,000 people across the globe, and stage fright has never been a factor.

It may be because I adore telling any and everyone about my interests. It could also be due to the fact that my audience and I remain separated by the glossy screens of laptops and smartphones.

Whichever the case, the ongoing journey of my YouTube channel (https://www.youtube.com/MissJoi100) has been one of my most valuable experiences since middle school. My passion for creating and sharing content for the world has only grown stronger as my subscribers blossomed from 10 to 10,000 people.

Committing to posting weekly advice, lifestyle, and fashion videos has allowed me to connect with my true love for all things journalism and media. From filling a plethora of notebooks with brainstorming ideas and goals, to taking hours to perfect the final edit of my next video, every aspect has been enjoyable.

The greatest satisfaction, however, is when I receive a message from someone I've helped—whether it be with advice on how to tackle difficult high school classes, or where to find cute, affordable back-to-school outfits. I strive to create content that I know others will be able to utilize and learn from. For example, my current series on college campus tours is aiding those who do not have the resources to travel outside of their state to do visits.

After almost seven years of talking to my camera for fun, my passion has only grown stronger. Excitement rests in my heart whenever I can click the post button for my next video. In the future, I desire to expand my audience from the thousands to the millions, but for now, I am just enjoying the journey.

YEARLY HIGH SCHOOL CHECKLIST

Freshman Year
- Try out new clubs, sports, and activities
- Earn great grades
- Schedule more difficult courses for your sophomore year

Sophomore Year
Fall
- Narrow down your extracurriculars to what you really love
- Consider starting a club if you cannot find an activity you enjoy
- Continue to receive great grades

Spring
- Schedule challenging courses (AP/IB/Honors) for your junior year
- Position yourself to attain leadership positions in your extracurriculars

Junior Year
Fall
- Take the SAT and ACT for the first time
- Run for leadership positions in your extracurriculars
- Write down 20 colleges you might be interested in, and start the research process
- Attend a college fair in your area
- Schedule college visits

Spring
- Ask for teacher recommendations
- Take second round of standardized testing
- Complete AP Exams
  Talk to your guidance counselor about your college inter-

* Introduce yourself to your college admissions officers through e-mail
* Schedule equally challenging courses for your senior year

Summer
* Create Common Application Account
* Read Common Application essay prompts
* Brainstorm essay ideas and start a rough draft
* Finalize college list
* Complete College Search Worksheets to narrow down school options
* Make a list of scholarships you wish to apply to

Senior Year

Fall
* Finish college essays and supplements
* Submit early applications
* Schedule or complete any admissions interviews
* Apply for scholarships

Spring
* Submit any remaining Regular Decision applications
* Complete financial aid forms
* Apply for scholarships
* Make your final your college decision and submit enrollment deposit
* Join your new class's Facebook group to connect with your peers

COLLEGE SEARCH WORKSHEET

(This PDF is available for download at JoiWade.com)

JoiWade.com/book

You Got Into Where?
College Application Checklist

School Name:	
City/State	
User ID + password	
Contact Person	

School Type	Safety	System Type	
	Range	Semester	
	Reach	Quarters	
Visit Date		Other	

Enrollment

Enrollment			
Undergraduates		Women %	
Post Graduates		Men %	
Total Students		Ethnic %	

Last Year's Profile

Last Year's Profile			
Acceptance Rate RD		Acc.R ED	
Graduation Rate		Average Aid	
Student-Faculty Ratio		% Receive Aid	
Mid 50% SAT		Mid 50% ACT	
Average GPA		Top 10%	

Application Details

Application Details		
Early Program Type		
	App. Deadline	Notification Date
Early Program		
Regular Decision		
Application Fee		
Common App	YES	NO
Writing Supp	YES	NO

Application Materials

Application Materials	Date Due:	Submitted:
App Complete		
Transcript		
SAT/ACT		
Letters Required		
Mid Year Report		
School Profile		
FAFSA		
AP Scores		
Final Transcript		
Interview? Yes/ No and Date		

AP Credits

Subject	My Score	Needed Score	Credits Gained

Interested Majors

Interested Majors	Check if Applies
	Study Abroad
	Internships
	Minority Recr
	Ranking

STUDENT FAQS

1. How do I figure out my chances of being admitted to a certain school?

There is no surefire way to figure out whether you will be admitted to a school or not. Admissions decisions remain a mystery, no matter how much the process is deciphered. However, you can get a feel for whether your credentials are academically up to par with other previously admitted students.

Google-search the school's "freshman profile" to find things like average GPA and test scores. Use this as a way to measure up yourself to other students. Do not be discouraged if you do not fall in line. If you have other desirable traits like a ton of AP courses or unique extracurriculars, you may still have a chance for admissions. However, be knowledgeable that the freshman profile represents a large portion of the students that the school is admitting.

2. What do I do if I am changing high schools?

I moved to a different state the summer before my senior year. This worried me, because I had no idea how it would factor into my college admissions. If you recently changed high schools it is important to build a relationship with your new guidance counselor as soon as you begin school. Your guidance counselor is going to have to write a recommendation on your behalf and send important information such as transcripts to your colleges, so having that relationship from the beginning will make the process a lot easier.

Also, consider receiving recommendation letters from teachers and previous guidance counselors from your old school if you are moving after your sophomore year.

3. How do I choose between two essay ideas?

If you are stuck choosing between multiple essay ideas, I recommend creating an outline for each essay. This will allow you to plan out each essay and see if you have enough supporting details to create an impressive manuscript. Ask friends and family which essay illustrates you as a person the best. See if one essay exemplifies your dedication to education, leadership abilities, or a time you showed strength in the face of adversity. After thinking into the details, you should have a better idea of which essay works best. If you are still in love with your unused idea, consider using it for a supplement as a short-answer question. You can also use it for scholarship applications.

4. What if my parents are leaving paying for college up to me?

Many students are left with the financial burden of college on their shoulders. It is important to think ahead if you are in this situation. As early as possible, start planning things like getting a job and applying for scholarships. Read books and articles about people who have paid for their own education and how they did it. Talk with other students whom you know are paying for their college tuition, and see what they are doing to help offset the costs.

5. What if my parents do not want me to go out of state for college?

If your parents have told you that you can only go to a school that is inside of your state and you are considering other schools, it is important to see their perspective. Is their concern out-of-state costs, or the distance? Remind your parents that many students do not pay the cover price to attend private institutions. Ask if you can still apply to a few out-of-state schools to see what they award you for scholarships and financial aid. See if you have any family that lives in the state you are considering moving to, in order to help your parents feel at case.

Finally, see if you can afford to take a campus visit, so your parents can see the environment you could be living in.

6. What should I do if I do not have a phenomenal GPA or grades?

Your academic record is a huge factor in your college admissions. However, some students have a rough year that brings down their GPA, and they are concerned as to how it will factor in their admissions decisions. If you do not have phenomenal grades, make sure that your college list has schools that match you academically. You want to attend a school you can be successful in.

After you find some schools that match your credentials, make sure you work hard to improve your grades up until college application time. Dedicate time to your extracurriculars as well, especially if you have a special talent in sports or the arts. Also, think of powerful essay topics that illustrate who you are as a student both inside and outside of the classroom.

7. *What if my test scores are not up to par?*

Many students get hung up on standardized test scores. While not everyone is a great test-taker, you can think ahead of time so you can study, prepare, and earn the best scores possible. Once you have all of your scores back and deadlines start to arrive, you must think of how else you can illustrate yourself as a desirable student, whether that is with a unique activities list, powerful recommendations, or a one-of-a-kind essay.

8. *Should I apply to a school I cannot afford?*

Students should apply to a variety of schools to make their college list as flexible as possible. Apply to public and private institutions, in-state and out-of-state schools, "reach" and "safety" schools, and affordable and not-so-affordable schools. As explained before, many times the price that students end up paying for college is less than the cost listed on admissions websites. Many Ivy League institutions now have programs that only award need-based aid in the form of grants that do not have to be paid back.

9. *Do AP exams count?*

AP exams do not count toward your admissions unless you physically send your scores to each respective college. Most schools you apply to will not require you to send your scores. I recommend sending scores only if you have received a 4 or 5 on AP exams and you believe that would help you in your admissions.

10.Why can't I finish all of the SAT/ACT in time?

One of the top problems students have with standardized testing is not figuring out how to answer the questions, but figuring out how to answer them in time. The only surefire way to improve your pacing with the exams is to take timed practice tests. Start by taking them section-by-section until you eventually are ready to take a full practice exam. As you do more practice, you will learn how much time you have to answer your questions, and your pacing should improve greatly.

ADMISSIONS INTERVIEW FAQS

1. What made you want to apply to our University/College?

It is very possible that the interviewer will question why you have interest in their institution in the first place. They are hoping that you will bring up unique aspects about the college and not general pamphlet sayings. For example, for someone applying to New York University, they should focus their answer their question regarding the University, not how they would love to see Broadway shows on the weekends.

2. What activity on your resume are you most proud of?

This question is asked in order to figure out what you care about and have spent your time with during your time in high school. I recommend mentioning an activity that you have had a long-term commitment to (3-4 years of high school) and hopefully have a leadership position in. If you started any initiatives or hosted any events, this would be a great time to talk about the work you put into those. Use this time to show and not tell; use specific anecdotes so that the interviewer can really grasp what type of person you are.

3. What would you take advantage of during your time enrolled here?

Here is another question where it would be nice to have done your research. Before your interview, look up specific things about the school like courses offered, notable professors, and clubs you would be interested in joining or even starting. Make sure you link things that you have done in high school to things you wish to continue to do in college. Also, do not stray away from academics. Admissions officers want students that love to learn on their campuses as well.

4. During your high school career, when have you shown leadership?

Colleges are also looking for students that possess leadership qualities to enroll in their institutions. During the interview, you are going to want to explain and not list things that just are on your resume. Of course being a president of a club requires leadership, however, it is much more effective to provide an example of a specific instance where your leadership shined best. Before your interview think through some pinnacle times during your education or club involvement that you really expressed leadership qualities.

MY FAVORITE RESOURCES ON ADMISSIONS AND SCHOLARSHIPS:

Books:

- *adMISSION POSSIBLE* by Majorie Hansen Shaevitz

- *A is for Admission* by Michele A. Hernandez, Ed.D.

- *Confessions of a Scholarship Winner* by Kristina Ellis

- *The Ultimate Scholarship Book* by Gen Tanabe

- McGraw Hill's *10 ACT Practice Tests*

Blogs:

- "CollegeAppChick," Tumblr (collegeapp-chick.tumblr.com)

- "The Choice Blog," *New York Times* (thechoice.blogs.ny-times.com)

Websites:

- *Scholly,* Scholarship Search (myscholly.com/#scholly)

- *BigFuture* by the College Board (bigfuture.collegeboard.org)

- *College Confidential*, discussion website (collegeconfidential.com)

- *The Princeton Review*, Test prep, tutoring, college rankings

YouTube Channels

- *MissJoi100* (youtube.com/user/MissJoi100)

- *Katherout* (youtube.com/user/MyPreppyStyle)

TIPS FOR PARENTS HELPING THEIR CHILDREN APPLY TO COLLEGE

I suggest that parents research the college application process if they are not familiar with the basic fundamentals. A good way to start is by reading this book! There are also tons of parent blogs, videos, and other resources to familiarize yourself with the process.

On the College Search

You will find that your student's college list will change constantly. What may be their number-one school in the beginning may not even make the list of schools they are applying to come fall of their senior year. While it is great to suggest schools your student should look into, make sure you give your student space to explore and find the right college fit. Help your student plan campus tours and visits around school breaks and vacations. Look into your contacts to see if you know any school alumni or alumnae who would be willing to talk to your student about their undergraduate experiences.

On Testing

Do not pressure your student about test scores close to their SAT/ACT test date. Your student needs to be confident and have as little stress as possible going into the test. Help your student to register for the exams and keep track of deadlines and test dates. The evening before the exam, make sure you student gets a good night's sleep. The morning of the exam, make sure they get a good breakfast, and offer to drive them to the test.

On Applications and Essays

Make sure that your student is completing the applications, and that you are merely a proofreader. Make sure all of the important information—the student's name, address, e-mail address, phone number, Social Security number, etc.—is entered correctly. Try to intervene as little as possible with the essay writing process; admissions officers can usually tell when a parent, not a student, has written a college essay. But feel free to offer your ideas and editing services as much as you would like.

On Financial Details

From the beginning you should discuss with your student how much you will be able to contribute to their college tuition. The costs start to add up as early as senior year: college visits, testing fees, and application costs can total hundreds or even thousands of dollars. After those fees are covered, you must think ahead to the next four years of your student's education. Help your student search for scholarships that can defray the costs of tuition. See if your job offers scholarships as well. Also, don't forget that many times families end up paying significantly less than the cover price that schools list on their websites. So do not take a school off your child's college list until you see its final financial aid packages.

ADVICE FROM RECENTLY ADMITTED STUDENTS

I took the time to ask students admitted to amazing schools to give their advice to the readers of this book.

There really is no magic combination when applying to competitive schools or scholarships. Keep in mind the kind of students the school attracts so you can gauge whether or not you want to go there, but don't put too much stock in being a certain "type' of student. Know that you're uniquely amazing and trust that the admissions committee will pick up on that in your application.

— Morenike Ibidapo, Vanderbilt University,
Class of 2020

I think what makes an applicant stand out is not only grades and SAT scores but their commitment to other activities. A lot of students will have great ECs, too, so what differentiates a person from another will be their level of commitment and sincerity in whatever they're doing. Also, essays are very, very, very important, and they give you a chance to show the college what you come from and how you want to use your college education. They don't expect us to be clear and set for life after these four years; they just want to see our passion to do something worthwhile and good with the education they're providing. (And, on top of this, you still need good grades and scores to increase your chances).

— Hridee, University of Southern California, Class of 2020

Interviews: Be on time and bring your best self. This is the time to confidently (not arrogantly) express all your achievements and aspirations. Ensure that there is a connection between the things you say. This connection should be made by you and not the interviewer. Use this as a time to fill in the gaps of your essays and resume.

— Antasia Glenn, University of Pennsylvania,
Class of 2019

Honestly, I would say the biggest thing is work hard. What sets you apart from the other thousands of applicants will not be your grades alone. It's the classes you take and whether you are challenging yourself. It's how involved you are in jobs, sports, extracurricular activities, and volunteer opportunities, in addition to a heavy school load that will show you off as a hard worker. A good ACT/SAT score doesn't hurt, either. Although the stressful tests, the all-nighters, the mental breakdowns, and your constant staying in to finish that last homework assignment before the deadline is difficult to do, especially your senior year, it will all be worth it in the end when the college you want to go to most sees that too.

— Tehillah Alphonso, University of Southern California,
Class of 2020, Popular Music Performance major

I'd encourage them to apply to a lot of scholarships, even if they don't think that they'll get them. Apply to scholarships worth small amounts of money, and it'll add up and really help in the long run. Private schools, like Northwestern, or any high-ranking school with a large endowment will make it possible for you to attend despite your financial situation. They have money

for scholarships and financial aid, and they are willing to give it out to students. Apply to schools you're interested in, and they'll let you know how they can help.

— Maya Armstrong, Northwestern University,
Class of 2019

As someone who was admitted to the school of art and design, I would say the portfolio (if your major/application requires one) is critical. Obviously to get into a school like USC you need to have strong grades and test scores, but beyond that, the portfolio is what's going to help you stand out. Choose pieces that truly show the breadth of your talent. If you work in different mediums, showcase that in what you submit. Show that you paint, draw, and sculpt! If you only work in one medium, you can still show a wide range of skill/experience. My portfolio was all photography, but I included color and black & white, digital and darkroom, portrait and landscape, et cetera. I also chose pieces that reflect my unique style as an artist, so that the admissions officers could really get to know me as an artist. Basically, a portfolio should be a really comprehensive overview of your skills and talents.

— Emma Masterson, University of Southern California
Roski School of Art and Design, Class of 2020

The college application process is not nearly as stressful as it seems. It goes over SO quickly. I was blessed enough to be nominated to receive a full-tuition scholarship from 1 of 5 colleges. After a three-round interview process, I was selected along with 10 other students from my state to receive the scholarship to the George Washington University. Display of

leadership, academic achievement, and good character helped me to gain this award.

— Breesa Bennett, Posse Scholar, George Washington University, Class of 2020

What I think set me apart from other applicants was what I wrote about in my essays. It is important to have good grades and good test scores, but, although I am a good student, so is everyone else that gets accepted into USC, but I wrote about topics very specific to my life and what I thought would make me stand out the most. For example, I wrote about how I trained puppies for two years, which I felt like was something different from normal after-school activities. I also wrote my Common Application essay about ignorance and connected it to my life. I think it is important to make your application personal and not general.

— Pearl Owei, University of Southern California, Class of 2020, Psychology major

One of the most important realizations I had during the college admission process was that colleges don't solely look at your GPA and SAT scores. Until they read your essays and examine your extracurricular interests, you're only a number in the system. Once they hear your true voice and learn what kind of person you are, you then transform from a number to a human being and a possible future student. Because of this, it's important to utilize your time during high school to participate in activities that interest YOU. Try to discover your passion, while also helping others. Try to make a difference in your community, and try to find yourself. If you do this, you will become a better

person, whether or not you are admitted to the selective university.

—Anthony Aguilar, University of
Southern California, Class of 2020

The biggest piece of advice I could give to a high-school student is to get your name out there early. You'll find that your e-mails are answered a little bit faster and with more personalized information that way. Yes, your admissions rep will help everyone, but any rep will be a little more willing to take an extra step to get things done for a student they are familiar with and know wants to go to their school. I figured out my dream school (USC) the end of my sophomore year and almost immediately began getting into contact with my admissions rep. A year and a half later, she guided me through the application process and gave me real advice on what to expect and which steps to take, not just the generic statements she gives to everyone.

Aside from making yourself a familiar face, I'd say definitely take your schooling seriously. There are so many people who early on in high school know what they want to do, but everyone changes their mind, and you don't want to be stuck with little to no options.

Last, just relax. Make yourself a cup of tea, don't procrastinate, and breathe.

— Alyssa Sibley, University of Southern California,
Class of 2020

Make sure the college knows why they want you and vice versa. Describe how you would fit into that school culture, what opportunities does that school offer that you would take advantage of, and how amazing of a fit you are for that school and that school is for you. Also

(and this might just be because USC is really focused on interdisciplinary work), I think colleges really want someone who brings a unique perspective or personality to their academic program and to their class. In my own essays, I talked about a project I did with my friends about audio processing and how USC could give me the opportunities I needed to extend my project. Computer Science is a really popular major, but I think the inclusion of music and music technology made my application more interesting—so include some sort of creative factor into your essays! It might be difficult to think of one right away, because it obviously differs from person to person, but it's something I think really helped my application. And at the end of the day, if a college doesn't accept you, it's not the end of the world. The college that accepts you is the best college for you!

— *Melissa Wen, University of Southern California, Class of 2020, Computer Science major*

Colleges are so arbitrary, and you will never know what will happen. Some people try to find that perfect formula to get into a top college, but, to be honest, there is no one correct way to do so. Show the colleges who you are, not only through what you did for your school, but also what you have achieved through your progression/development through the years and your aspirations. Grades, GPA, and SAT scores are just slices of a whole pie that colleges take in account. The essay portion is where you can truly let your personality shine. I opened up to the writing part of the application, because I realized that whoever is behind the screen reading my application won't care about what I did and what I said in the long term; it's what sets you apart that they care about.

Try and find your passion in what you love to do, and through that, you are able to discover your purpose, and that's what colleges look to see. That you were able to find something you are passionate about and explore whilst showing that you care about school.

Most importantly, start on your application early on in the summer so that you can review every piece of your application later on, and so you can give yourself time to apply for scholarships!

Good luck with everything, and just remember: it's not the college you go to that defines you, it's what you will be able to do at the place you end up that establishes who you will become, and will essentially pave the way for your successful future.

—Alex Van, University of Southern California, Class of 2020, Human Biology Major

Just a quick tip: When I was completing my junior year, I got a lot of e-mails about week-long summer exposure camps at various colleges like Johns Hopkins, Harvard and Brown. I thought that these were not worth the money (some cost upwards of $5K for a single week), so I did not attend. Several people I know did, however, and most of them ended up being admitted to those schools, even though they were "reach schools" for them. So, my advice would be if you are 100% certain on a university and you are worried about getting in, seriously consider signing up for one of those programs at that school.

—Anish Mahadeo, University of Southern California, Class of 2020

One of the things that helped me the most in getting through the nitty-gritty of college application season was preparing ahead of time. I started looking up the Common Application personal statement prompts for the coming year and the specific, unique prompts of each school I was thinking about applying to, and I started brainstorming and writing down whatever came to mind. This helped me zero in on some core ideas later on, even if I only got a sentence or two out of a big paragraph of draft writing. Focusing on what applies to your own life is important, but you don't have to be a superstar in high school to write about yourself and make yourself stand out. I've been involved in many extracurriculars in high school that helped form my essays, but I also focused on instances where I learned a lesson, or a time when my perspective changed because of an event in my life. In the end, pacing yourself is the best way to tackle the monumental workload and time consumption that is college applications.

— Anastasia Barbato, University of Southern California ,
Class of 2020

STUDENT STORY: ON CHOOSING THE RIGHT MATCH

I live about an hour away from my high school. Every time I tell someone that, they look at me like I am crazy.

"Why would you go through that hassle every day?" is the usual question asked.

I often wondered that myself, but my parents and I knew that it would be a 60-minute ride to change my reality, as my private school was one of the finest in the state. My parents also had big hopes for me, as they believed that my unique background and circumstances would lead to a greater opportunity for me.

So when my Columbia letter came at the end of March, I thought I had finally reached what they had driven miles and miles for. However, after my initial shock and joy of finally reaching this goal for the best, I realized that I did not wish to attend Columbia University. It is not that I was not grateful to be accepted, it is just that I had fallen in love with another school, Howard University.

Howard does not have the clout or resources on the same level as Columbia, but when I stepped foot on campus it felt like home, something I had never experienced before due to my isolation at my small private school. Of course, because I had worked so hard, I knew that my work was deserving to be at a prestigious institution like Columbia. However, I realized that, although Columbia had everything I wanted academically, it did not have what I needed mentally.

Columbia would make me smart, but Howard would make me strong. And the greatest thing I had gained from my experience at my unconventional high school is that money and prestige does not make the person—it is how good they are to the world that makes them the best people.

So, I do not need Columbia to be "twice as good," because I have a community at Howard that can build me up to be an even greater service to humanity.

— Nahlah Abdur-Rahman, Howard University, Class of 2020

ABOUT THE AUTHOR

Joi Wade is enrolled in the University of Southern California's Class of 2020. Born in Maryland and raised in Pennsylvania, Joi developed a passion for writing and media from an early age. In middle school, she began to produce videos for her own YouTube channel. Her family moved from Pennsylvania to Georgia in her senior year of high school. During this time, Joi began to shift the focus of her YouTube channel to videos on the college admissions process.

As a first-generation college student, Joi worked hard to ensure she would not be at a disadvantage when applying to her choice colleges and universities. Her long nights of hard studying and writing college essays were all worth it when she received acceptances to her dream schools.

Joi did not realize the powerful effect her videos would have on their viewers until she began to receive daily advice inquiries from other high-school students about the college admissions process. This high demand impelled her to continue to offer her advice through her YouTube videos. This also inspired her to offer ACT and college advisory services as well.

Joi began to draft her first college admissions book at the end of her college application and admission process. She wishes to write more published works in the future and to expand her YouTube audience and video portfolio.

Outside of writing and video production, Joi enjoys photography, graphic design, and traveling.

Visit Joi's website, www.joiwade.com, for FREE downloadable PDF's on college admissions topics not covered in this book!

Connect with Joi:

Website: JoiWade.com
YouTube: YouTube.com/MissJoi100
Twitter: @JoiKWade
Instagram:@JoiKWade

To contact Joi for speaking opportunities, media requests, or interviews, please send an e-mail to:
joiwadeinquiries@gmail.com

If you enjoyed this book, will you consider sharing the message with others?

- Recommend this book to any high-school freshman, sophomore, junior or senior who will soon be going through the college application process.

- Share this book with your school guidance counselor so he or she can recommend it to other students.

- Mention the book on a Twitter update, Instagram photo, Facebook post, or blog post, using the hashtag #GotIntoWhereBook.

- Order a copy of this book for someone you know who would be challenged and inspired by its message.

- Submit a testimonial on JoiWade.com.

- Submit a review of the book on Amazon and iBooks.

You can subscribe to Joi's e-mail list at: JoiWade.com.

Made in the USA
Monee, IL
29 August 2019